Getting it Together

Getting it Together

DILEMMAS FOR THE CLASSROOM

BASED ON KOHLBERG'S APPROACH

Beverly A. Mattox

Published by

PENNANT PRESS

San Diego, California 92120

10 9 8

Last number is printing number

ISBN 0-913458-24-4

Cover design by James Michael Brown

Printed in the United States of America

To my mother,
for imparting protective beauty
and sweet memories
to the pages of my life.

ACKNOWLEDGMENTS

I wish to thank the following persons for their help in the development and writing of this book:

Mrs. Margo Koryda, who provided many of the moral dilemmas and served as a sounding board for ideas.

Mrs. Dorothy Rich, Director of the Home-School Institute, for believing I should write this book.

Mr. James Luster, publisher, for his patience and support during the writing.

Mrs. Beth Boisseau and Dr. Ruth Clay for their help in editing.

Mrs. Betty Chilton of the Fairfax County Professional Library for information and help.

And my family who provided assistance in so many ways.

Also, I offer my sincere thanks to my professional colleagues and friends, who had the faith to believe this book would one day be written.

Beverly Mattox

TO THE READER

This book has been prepared to provide the working-level educator with an understanding of what the Kohlberg approach is and how to use it in the classroom.

Every effort has been made to interpret Dr. Kohlberg's work faithfully. Since Dr. Kohlberg's writings are seemingly directed toward the graduate student at the university level, this book may appear to be a great simplification. We trust that it is not an over-simplification.

Getting It Together is intended to serve as a primer, a readily understood starting point for working with a very helpful approach to moral education.

We hope you find it useful.

The Publisher

TABLE OF CONTENTS

1

A Brief Introduction to the Kohlberg Approach

Educators find that they are able to help students grow in their ability to make moral choices by using the approach to values and moral development developed by Dr. Lawrence Kohlberg of Harvard University.

In Dr. Kohlberg's approach a climate is established in which students experience and practice moral choices. The students utilize their own thinking and that of their peers in their growth process. By discussing and role-playing the "real moral dilemmas" that crop up in everyday living they are exposed to their peers' moral reasoning. They talk with one another, argue, compare and naturally move up a scale of improved morality. There is no sermonizing on a "bag of virtues."

Peer group interaction, primarily discussion and role-playing, is employed to help students move upward from one stage to the next. Kohlberg does not attempt to foster a specific set of values, but believes students should work at their own development through peer group interaction. The teacher presents a dilemma or problem situation. The students discuss or role-play the dilemma. They draw from their experiences to solve the problem. In this active process students join their concern for others, for justice and for equality into a set of morals that work for them.

Kohlberg bases moral education on universal principles of justice, independent of a specific religious tradition. Moral education in the school, in his view, should be fundamentally a doctrine of justice. It should involve natural principles of justice which guide all societies and which we know by reason. While making justice central to moral education, Kohlberg notes that moral education can include the development of religious faith. However, he holds that it is possible to teach moral education independently of religious education.

Kohlberg's method is based on the following ideas:

1. **Morality develops in stages.** When basic values appear to be different, it is because we are at different levels of maturity in thinking

about moral issues.

2. **Everyone passes through the same stages of moral development.** Students move through the stages at different rates. Stages cannot be skipped. Some reach higher stages than others at adulthood.

3. **Moral reasoning is related to behavior.** Students with better reasoning ability are more likely to act in a moral way. Students who base their morals on the welfare of others are more likely to do the "right" things than students whose motives are based on avoiding punishment, the reasoning of a lower stage.

The students' interaction with their environment is crucial. As they begin to fit together their social experiences and understand the interrelationships, learning occurs. Often students make very different decisions and yet have the same basic moral values.

4. Discussion is needed for moral growth. Kohlberg believes the discussion process can help students move to higher levels of moral reasoning. Discussion stimulates ways of thinking that are natural for the students. Through discussion students see the limits of their reasoning. They compare the reasons of

other students. Conflicting views force students to evaluate their own morality.

Kohlberg's method provides the educator with a step-by-step description of moral development. With this framework teachers are able to tell which stages of reasoning a group of students expresses, and are then able to plan suitable interaction for assisting moral growth.

Kohlberg defines a framework of six universal stages of moral development. He further groups the stages into three levels, two stages per level. These are the **Pre-Conventional Level**(stages one and two), the **Conventional Level**(stages three and four) and the **Post-Conventional Level**(stages five and six). Easy-to-remember descriptions of the orientation of each of the stages are listed below:

Stage One: **"Avoid punishment"**

Stage Two: **"Self-benefit"**

Stage Three: **"Acceptance by others"**

Stage Four: **"Maintain the social order"**

Stage Five: **"Contract fulfillment"**

Stage Six: **"Ethical principle"**

It has been observed that 70 percent of all Americans operate on the Conventional Level, at the upper end of stage three and the lower end of stage four.

It appears that in order to use the Kohlberg approach to the best advantage, teachers should have their own emotional houses in order. Teachers who have developed self-awareness can more readily understand their students. Experience has shown that teachers who are the most successful are those who work with an understanding of the child as a "whole" person, including the cognitive, affective and the psycho-motor aspects of behavior.

2

Some Reasons for Moral Education

Students have many facts at their commands. For these facts to be useful, students should be able to use them to enrich their everyday lives. Moral education can help integrate facts with meaningful applications to living.

One reason for moral education is to help students understand themselves and their society. This includes learning to accept individuality and uniqueness, and to build on these to mature self-hood. Students need to understand the relationships between people and their environment. They need to understand the relationships between values and behavior. They need meaningful and valid values for themselves in order to be able to function successfully within society. To this end, students need to learn to clarify value issues and solve problems.

Another reason for moral education is to help students become active citizens. Students must be aware of how to use their education in participating in society. They need opportunities to apply their learning in real situations. The class should be seen by both the teacher and the students as a mini-society in which to develop this awareness and to practice behavior.

Students need to talk about their feelings and be exposed to the feelings of others. Through interaction with others, students learn that the differences between themselves and others are not as great as the similarities. They discover that other students experience feelings of uncertainty, self-consciousness and rejection. Ultimately, students gain an understanding of themselves. Ideally, acceptance of self and others will follow.

In the past sone teachers felt that helping students understand their lives and solve their problems interfered with the subject disciplines, normally the first priority of school. But teachers are beginning to feel that the opposite may be true. Subject discipline and cognitive learning is usually increased when such learning touches the student's life directly.

The development of skills in acquiring and evaluating facts to solve problems are essential parts of moral education. Decision-making itself involves complex reasoning processes. These same skills and processes help students in subject matter areas. Learning is also enhanced through the student's active participation in role-playing, class discussion, decision-making and problem-solving activities. Such maximum attention and involvement lead to effective learning.

The Kohlberg framework explored in this book is relevant for today's students. It can help students discover what is meaningful to them, how values influence their actions, and the importance of decision-making based upon careful examination of issues.

Successful moral education will assist the students' growth in moral reasoning. It will educate them to make full use of the values each has developed. And, ideally, it will equip them to function at the levels of morality to which each has grown.

3

The
Educator's Opportunity

Educators cannot evade the questions of values. Values influence actions, motivate behavior and determine life-styles. They play a vital role in decision-making. Values are real and relevant. They are reflected in the judgements we make and the solutions we choose. Values help us weigh alternatives and order priorities.

Schools should help students examine, develop and rationally choose their values. Students need help with sorting through the conflicting values of television, newspapers, peers and parents. Students need to judge these values for themselves.. And they need to feel good about their own decisions and behaviors. Students must process society's confusing signals in a way that will let them live with themselves and interact with others.

To help students make decisions about values, educators should emphasize reasoning, inquiry and critical thinking. These are the basic tools for making sense out of experience. Combined with problem-solving strategies, fundamental concepts and academic disciplines, these processes help students evaluate their experiences and put those experiences into a rational whole.

This book develops the "dilemma" discussion approach to peer group interaction. Motivation, presentation, trial and insight are the steps in this teaching method. The discussion technique enables students to make choices and evaluate consequences in the society of their peers. Essential to this approach is the use of the classroom as a "laboratory" for personalized learning. Students are actively involved in using their increased self-knowledge to make choices for themselves and to examine the problems of living.

Growth in the dimension of empathy is essential as well. Through discussion and role-playing students become aware of how others react in unfamiliar situations. They develop empathy for each other and learn new solutions to problem situations. They compare the outcomes of different solutions and see whether their behavior brings the desired result. In essence, the students compare the relationship between their behavior and their goals.

It follows, of course, that inquiry and empathy will flourish only when the classroom climate is warm and accepting. Identifying and deciding values is difficult when students fear the consequences. Students will develop intellectually when they are emotionally safe. Within such a climate, the techniques and strategies suggested in this book can be applied to learning situations to help students determine their feelings, attitudes and behaviors.

Clearly, the "dilemma" approach to moral discussion reflects a philosophy of teaching. The basic attitude must be one of trust. Students can be trusted to make wiser moral choices when they have the opportunity to examine moral issues. The emphasis on critical thinking skills as an alternative to blind acceptance of norms or authority. The teacher does not dictate or impose values, but instead helps the student develop a valuing system which will guide him toward intelligent, considered values and actions.

Since the teacher's task is one of encouraging students to identify values and value confiicts, it is the teacher's responsibility to lead students to behavior that will further their goals. The teacher works with students to "get it together" for themselves.

Teachers might continually ask themselves:

Do my students see the relation between the skills they learn and their own lives, present and future?

Am I concerned with the dignity and integrity of each student?

Do I teach subject areas, or do I teach students?

Do I teach students to set goals for themselves?

Do I teach for understanding?

Moral education can be pursued within the framework of the school. However, it requires insight, motivation, responsibility and empathy — the qualities and expertise of the truly professional educator.

4

Kohlberg's Stages of Moral Development

Kohlberg's stages of moral development help teachers recognize the levels of moral awareness in the classroom. Kohlberg has found that moral awareness develops in a sequence of stages. People in all cultures progress through the same sequence. Stages are sequential and cannot be skipped.

Kohlberg found a universal and natural sense of justice that was intuitively known by a child. The particular aspect of justice expressed is an evidence of the stage of moral growth. While movement through the stages is always toward a higher level of morality, progression is not automatic. Moral growth is facilitated as people interact with others. When students are exposed to discussion and the conflicting views of others, they have the opportunity to compare and draw new moral conclusions.

Kohlberg's first three stages describe a code of moral conduct based on external rewards and punishments, a **dependent** approach to behavior. In stages four through six, the moral reasons for behavior stem from personal beliefs and conscience, an **independent** approach to behavior.

The stages may also be classified by societal orientation. The first two stages describe a **pre-conventional** morality level. At these stages, people are less influenced by the accepted norms of society. The third and fourth levels have a **conventional** orientation level. Both of these levels are tied to social expectations of behavior. The fifth and sixth stages are at a **post-conventional** level. They support a morality which springs from personal conscience, not bound by convention.

In abbreviated form, the six stages of moral development are:

Stage 1 — **"Avoid Punishment"** orientation.

Stage 2 — **"Self-Benefit"** orientation.

Stage 3 — **"Acceptance by Others"** orientation.

Stage 4 — **"Maintain the Social Order"** orientation.

Stage 5 — **"Contract Fulfillment"** orientation.

Stage 6 — **"Ethical Principle"** orientation.

Kohlberg describes a **Premoral Stage** through which most students will have passed by the time they enter classrooms. At this stage, the person knows good as anything pleasant and bad as anything painful. Infants are premoral in their inability to understand rules, authority or consequences. Thus, there is no sense of obligation or of action in terms of "I should." The pleasure search is not impeded by any considerations whatsoever.

The six stages which Kohlberg outlines will more likely apply to school age children. The distinguishing characteristics of these stages are as follows:

Stage 1 — "Avoid Punishment" orientation:

At this stage persons respond to rules, and are concerned with:

— How authority will react.

— Whether they will be punished or rewarded.

— Whether they will be labeled "good" or "bad."

The physical consequences determine whether an action is good or bad. Decisions are based on a blind obedience to an external power in an attempt to avoid punishment or seek reward. Morality exists in actions rather than in persons and standards. The ultimate "wrong" is getting into trouble.

Stage Two — "Self-Benefit" orientation:

At Stage Two, persons realize that each individual has an idea of what is "right" or best. They are concerned with:

— The needs and motives of others.

— The idea that one good turn (or bad) deserves another.

Fairness and sharing are interpreted in a practical manner. Self-interest in the compelling motive.

Human relationships are built on the premise of exchanging favors or revenge. What is right is serving one's needs, or the needs of others for a "fair" return. What is "fair" is doing something for others if they reciprocate. Such naive "back-scratching" equality is based on exchange and reciprocity.

Stage Three — "Acceptance by Others" orientation:

People see what is "right" from another's point of view as well as from their own. They are concerned with what others think. They strive for behavior which pleases others. At this stage, people are influenced by:

— The feelings of others.

— What others expect and approve.

— Beliefs about what a virtuous person would do.

This is the morality of maintaining good relations and of conforming to the general will. People adopt the stereotyped images of acceptable majority behavior. For the first time, behavior is judged by intention, and we hear the familiar, "He meant well."

Stage Four — Maintain the Social Order" orientation:

People at Stage Four consider "right" from the perspective of what is best for society. They examine the consequences of their actions for the group and society. They value:

— "Doing their duty."

— Respect for authority.

— Preserving the social order for its own sake.

— Rules as determiners of "right" behavior.

— Fulfilling the requirements of authority and society.

Individuals obey rules for their intrinsic value. Moral decisions are based on fixed rules which are "necessary" to perpetuate the order of society. Laws and rules are right because they exist; they are obeyed without question.

Stage Four marks the beginning of a sense of sacredness of human life as part of the social, moral or religious order.

Stage Five — "Contract Fulfillment" orientation:

The individual respects impartial laws and agrees to abide by them. The society agrees to respect the rights of the individual. The U.S. Constitution and the Declaration of Independence are based on these principles.

Aside from what has been democratically accepted, morality is a matter of personal choice. Moral issues are solved by the passage of laws based on general principles, e.g., "The greatest good for the greatest number." People at Stage Five believe laws should be changed when they infringe on human convictions. Persons at this stage choose to change laws rather than break them when such change is possible. Where it is not possible, they may choose to disobey what they consider to be an unjust law and *willingly* suffer the consequences. This differs from the rigidity of Stage Four's "law and order" orientation.

Stage Five people define rights in terms of individual standards as sanctioned and codified by society. Outside of the legal area, personal agreement is the binding element of obligation.

Stage Six — "Ethical Principle" orientation:
Conscience is the directing agent at this stage. Respect for each person's individuality is paramount. The values are believed to be valid for all humanity. The individual complies with rules to avoid self-condemnation.

Thus, at Stage Six morality is a decision of conscience based on universal ethical principles. The action must be good in itself and consistent with these principles. The individual makes his or her decisions on the basis of these principles.

OTHER CONSIDERATIONS

Four factors influence decision-making at each stage. These are the **rules** orientation, the **pragmatic** orientation, the **justice** orientation and the **conscience** orientation. Each stage is a variation of these four orientations. At each stage the situation, one's purposes and the consequences of one's actions are weighed somewhat differently when making a decision.

It is only at stages five and six (the post-conventional level) that individuals act on the basis of principles. Only at this post-conventional level is there a demonstrable relationship between moral judgment and moral action. Right and wrong at other stages are judged by concrete consequences, acceptance by others or institutional allegiance. Only at stages five and six is there a commitment to the principles of equality and justice for their own intrinsic value. Morality or "what ought to be," is explained by those principles rather than by fear of consequences, need for approval, or what authority requires.

EXPLORING A SEVENTH STAGE

In the Spring of 1974, Kohlberg announced that he is exploring a Seventh Stage[†], one which might be described as a "Faith" orientation. This stage involves a person's resolution of the question,, "What is the ultimate meaning of life?"

This "Faith" orientation stage does not conflict with the principles developed through the first six stages. Rather, it integrates those stages and provides a perspective on life's ultimate meaning. In Stage Seven the individual advances from an essentially human to a cosmic point of view.

After Stage Six, the individual experiences despair. He or she has developed principles of justice, yet is faced with an unjust world. Moral philosophy cannot solve the dilemma.

With Stage Seven there is a modification to a wider view of life. Emphasis changes from the

[†]Dr. Kohlberg described this Seventh Stage, as well as his other stages, in a speech given in Cleveland, Ohio, April 1974 at the National Catholic Educational Association Convention. The speech may be obtained on cassette tape (Pennant Catalog No. 3013) from Pennant Educational Materials, San Diego, California 92120.

individual to the cosmos. Instead of self as the primary nucleus, the cosmos or the infinite becomes focal. The meaning of life is examined from this standpoint. Belief in a fundamental being, God, or independent reality is developed at Stage Seven.

Stage Seven appears to be achieved most often by those persons who have reached Stage Six in their early twenties. The faith dimension usually comes later in life and is crucial for those who have achieved the post-conventional level of moral awareness. With this stage comes the moral strength to act on the principles of justice in an unjust world. One achieves the peace of sensing oneself as a part of the infinite whole. Stage Seven entails unity with an independent reality beyond the self, and a resolution to the ultimate questions of life and death. This new stage is a true reflection of "Getting It Together."

5

Techniques for Growing

Moral awareness develops as students discuss openly and "try on" attitudes and behaviors. Several classroom strategies provide students the setting and freedom to do this. These teaching techniques have in common a high degree of student involvement and the opportunity to practice alternatives in an atmosphere where there is no single right answer *given* for all students to accept. The emphasis is on experiencing and experimenting. The culmination is reflection, deliberation and, sometimes, decision.

DILEMMAS

The dilemma is a brief scenario involving a conflict. Students make choices about how they would behave in the situation described.

Dilemmas usually involve moral reasoning and lend themselves particularly well to analysis in terms of Kohlberg's six stages. A teacher skilled in recognizing the stages of moral thinking will find dilemmas an important diagnostic tool.

More importantly, they serve as exercises which can help students, through experience and reflection, to grow and develop in moral thinking. They let the student practice decision-making and equip him with methods of evaluating choices.

The other teaching strategies described below can also be used with dilemmas. Sample dilemmas for various grade levels are presented in Chapter 8; Chapter 9 provides instructions for writing dilemmas.

FISH BOWL

Fish bowl is a discussion technique. A small circle of students is assembled in the center of a larger circle. One extra chair is placed in the smaller circle. The dilemma or topic is discussed by members of the small circle. The members of the larger circle listen. When they wish to make a contributation they move into the empty chair and ask to be recognized. After they make their statement or ask a question, they must vacate the seat and return to the larger circle. The members of the larger circle may be asked to record reactions, solutions, decisions, reasons and comments. The group leader remains outside the "fish bowl" and observes the interaction and determines the length of time for the exercise. The "fish bowl" technique helps students listen to each other, present alternative ways of thinking and choose a possible solution.

SIMULATION

Simulation is a strategy for creating an experience in a classroom which will parallel (or simulate) elements of real life experience. For example, a history class might conduct a constitutional convention in order to experience the personal and political dynamics of such events. As students represent various interests and work toward agreement via compromise, they develop an experiential (as opposed to merely academic) sense of how the American constitution came into being.

It is important to realize that students do not act out a pre-determined scenario. Rather, they create the events out of the needs and concerns that motivate them in the roles they play. A simulation is active and spontaneous within the structure of the situation being simulated.

In moral education the teacher might simulate a social setting, such as life in a black ghetto, in order to help students explore the dynamics of the situation. Thus, the student might learn the relationship between desperation and lawlessness, or between lack of money and lack of education as they cope with the factors that cause the conflicts.

Simulations attempt to reflect the real issues of society, and permit students to explore and analyze related experiences. They stimulate interaction and introspection.

Simulations allow for:

— Portraying realities without exposing the participants to all of the threats and anxieties of the real life situation.

— Experiencing results of undersirable behaviors while still having options for altering those behaviors.

— Expressing deeply personal feelings while protected by the "make believe" quality of the simulation.

— Interacting with others on significantly deep levels.

— Thinking, planning and relating creatively.

In essence, a simulation is an opportunity to practice a behavior, feel the feelings, experience the consequences — but not "for keeps." All mistakes, misjudgements, bad feelings are revocable. The lesson may be learned and the damage may be undone. Life, of course, operates a much stricter school.

ROLE-PLAYING

Simulations involve the structures and dynamics of societal systems. Role-playing is less comprehensive. Quite simply, students take on the role of another person. They pretend to think, feel and act like that person. Role-playing can be part of a simulation. For example, while studying the dynamics of negotiation, a student might role-play an angry labor leader. Or, simulations aside, one student might role-play an angry parent while another plays a defensive teen-ager.

Role-playing frequently features a conflict in which two persons (playing roles) attempt to work out a solution. Or it may simply involve students in experiencing the feelings of a moral dilemma. For example, in moral education a teacher might ask a student to role-play President Truman as he makes his decision to drop the atomic bomb on Japan. Thus, role-playing can utilize soliloquy as well as dialogue, or scenes with many characters.

Role-playing helps students to:

— Explore several alternatives with no predetermined outcome.

— Explore emotions which are sometimes hidden.

— Express feelings safely in the guise of someone else.

— Develop tolerance for social differences.

— Develop acceptance of the ideas and feelings of other persons by portraying their point of view.

The following are suggestions for implementing roleplaying strategies:

1. Remind students that they must decide how the situation will end, and that more than one solution might be desirable.

2. Choose students to play roles with which they have identified through their comments.

3. Involve the audience by asking them to decide whether what they observe is fantasy or possibility, what the consequences might be for all the characters involved, and what alternative solutions might be proposed.

4. Follow up the role-playing with discussion of the audience's observations and the players' feelings and opinions.

5. Re-play the scenes if students have suggested alternatives.

6. Encourage students to apply the role-playing situation to their own lives if it seems useful to them and they are willing to do so.

6

The Teacher's Task

The wisest theories, the soundest approaches, the best materials still depend for implementation on the expertise of the teacher. The teacher's skill as group process facilitator, as a determiner of classroom climate, as a trouble-shooter and evaluator are essential to the success of moral education.

THE TEACHER'S ORIENTATION

The teacher's sense of purpose is the starting point. The teacher must work toward *stimulating* moral development, as opposed to indoctrinating students. This precludes telling students what to think, manipulating students to adopt the teachers preferences, modifying students' behavior so they do what teachers want.

Rather, teachers facilitate the students' development through a natural progression of stages. This individualized approach to moral development allows the teacher to view the student as a unique person and to allow the student to grow morally at his own pace.

The focus of Kohlberg's approach is the *student's search* rather than the *teacher's answers*. The teacher's function is to stimulate the searching and growth process.

The teacher as facilitator tries to build the individuals with whom he or she works into a cohesive group. The depth and quality of students' interactions with each other will have a strong bearing on the depth and quality of their explorations in moral reasoning. Thus, the teacher attempts to develop the following characteristics of successful groups:

1. The group thinks of itself as a unit. Members know each other by name and cooperate for identified goals.

2. Members understand the purpose of the group.

3. The group develops standards which guide its actions.

4. Participation is widespread though some members may contribute more than others. Attempts are made to include all members in discussion.

5. The atmosphere is accepting and friendly. Each group member feels a part of the group.

6. Leadership is shared among group members.

7. The talents of group members are utilized whenever possible.

8. There is continuous evaluation of goals, organization, attitudes and patterns of interaction.

9. There is unity within the group. Group members respect individual differences, but act as a unit when making decisions. There is loyalty, vitality and harmony characterizing the group as opposed to just a collection of individuals.

For some teachers this may involve a shift in stance. No longer is the teacher the actor and the students the audience. Instead, the teacher becomes part of the group. The teacher joins the group as a person and not as an authority.

The focus shifts from the accumulation of facts to thought processes. It shifts, too, from the intellect of the student to his unified being. The area of concern broadens to include the child in his life outside as well as inside school. Short term, measurable learning goals must make room for concentration on the teacher's year-long task of helping the student take responsibility for his own behavior and decisions.

THE TEACHER AS FACILITATOR

Essential as a proper orientation is, the teacher needs more. Certain specific skills in facilitating group processes can mean the difference between success and failure.

During class discussions and role-playing the teacher should attempt the following:

1. Insure that the processes of group thinking are based on the inquiry approach. Let the students solve the problem by asking questions.

2. Summarize important concepts and generalizations drawn from the discussion.

3. Maintain focus on the problem or situation and not on individual group members.

4. Plan lessons for sequential advancement to higher levels of moral thinking and skill in problem-solving.

5. Adapt to student differences in ability, knowledge, background and interest.

6. Intervene when the group strays from meaningful exploration.

7. Take a back seat if it makes the discussion flow freely.

The following system for probing answers has been developed by Miller and Vincour[†].They suggest the teacher help students clarify value terms with the following questions:

What do you mean by . . . ?

Could you state that another way?

Please give me some examples of that.

Can you define . . . ?

Can you be more specific?

Are you implying . . . ?

When requesting additional evidence the teacher might ask:

On what evidence do you base your judgments?

What makes you feel that way?

What evidence do you have to support that?

How do you know that?

What reasons do you have for believing . . . ?

The teacher should help students recognize the personal consequences of their solutions as well as society's possible reaction. The following questions may be helpful in testing solutions against existing conditions in the community.

Can this be interpreted in a different way?

Are there other alternatives?

[†]For a fuller development of this method, see "A Method for Clarifying Value Statements in the Social Studies Classroom," by Harry G. Miller and Samuel M. Vincour (1972, Erie Document Ed-070687).

What does this mean for society?

Who will it primarily affect?

Does this solution encourage better relatioı.ɔhips?

THE CLASSROOM CLIMATE

The classroom is best conceived as a learning laboratory for students to examine ideas and make their own decisions. The emphasis is on weighing, evaluating and sometimes practicing alternatives before drawing conclusions. These processes are very personal, and as such, they may be threatening. Students will not risk revealing very much of their inner selves if they can expect blame, censure or criticism. The students need warm, receptive listening. Only then will they feel safe enough to risk sharing feelings.

Toward this end, the teacher's task is two-fold. He or she must achieve sufficient rapport with individual students so that they feel safe and comfortable in that relationship. And teachers must also guide students toward the kind of caring, accepting behavior toward each other which will assure safety from insensitive remarks.

Communication will be enhanced if the room's seating arrangement permits students to see each other. Teachers may accomplish this by means of the circle, semicircle or oval, or by experimenting with whatever clusters help students to share thoughts and feelings with each other. Sometimes small group involvements will help students feel more at ease. The group should be large enough to provide stimulation but small enough to allow all members to participate.

The teacher should be aware of the complex social interactions within the classroom. There are at least two systems of interaction among students — an external one which probably includes the teacher and an internal arrangement at the peer level. If the teacher's insight can encompass the internal dynamics, he or she can promote better communication. An alert teacher might change the composition of a discussion group or re-structure a role-playing session based on an awareness of this level of interaction.

THE TEACHER AS TROUBLE-SHOOTER

Experience indicates that the approaches recommended above sometimes break down at certain points. The most persistent difficulties are domination of the discussion by a minority, the tendency to stray from pertinent issues and faltering debate.

The teacher can head off some of these problems by directing specific, answerable questions to the less verbal students. The greater the number of participants, the harder it is for a minority to dominate. (Of course, the teacher should be very careful not to be a dominating minority of one!) When comments are not germane to the issues, the teacher can re-focus the discussion.

Teachers need to support the person and his or her willingness to share without judging what he or she says. The students must be helped to grow and develop, to expand their moral reasoning by probing and exploring rather than through reinforcing desirable answers. The emphasis is on the person and the process.

THE TEACHER AS LEARNER

Teachers must know what they want to accomplish and be familiar with the methods available to them. Teachers must choose the of methods and materials to fit the needs of the students. In order to have a coherent, workable program of moral development, local decisions must be made regarding specific objectives, content, materials, teaching strategies and evaluation.

New teaching methods do not take effect overnight. A reasonable time is needed to plan and experiment, to become familiar with new materials and teaching techniques and to discover the ideas most suited to personal teaching styles and the responsiveness of students. If teachers are willing to experiment, learn and grow with their students, their patience and persistence will be greatly rewarded.

7

Using Dilemmas

The sample dilemmas presented in the following chapter are both diagnostic and growth tools. As such, they must be skillfully employed by the teacher. Used diagnostically, the dilemmas can reveal the moral stage at which the student is currently functioning. Used as growth tools, they can help students advance to thinking at the next higher stage.

To use the dilemmas to determine a given students level of functioning, the teacher will, of course, need to be thoroughly familiar with Kohlberg's stages. Then the teacher must listen to enough responses to determine the pattern of a student's thinking.

Kohlberg notes that an individual may respond on more than one stage of moral development. A student might apply more advanced moral reasoning to some situations than to others. Therefore, it is not possible to judge the student's moral maturity on the basis of a few statements. Frequent discussions involving moral conflicts are necessary for teacher to acquire an understanding of students' reasoning processes.

For example, replies to a series of ten dilemmas may indicate that a student falls between stages three and four. Perhaps on six of the dilemmas the individual responded with a stage three orientation and at stage four on the other four predicaments. Numerically, stage three dominates. Kohlberg considers the individual to be at the level of moral development indicated by the dominant stage.

A critical point for teachers to understand is that the particular solution a student chooses may not in itself reveal the stage of moral development. Until the *reasons* for choosing that solution have been explained; no determination of stage can be made. It is entirely possible that two students might choose the same resolution for a dilemma but for entirely different reasons.

One student might refrain from looting during a riot for fear of being shot. He would be reasoning at the Stage One "Avoid Punishment" level. Another student might choose not to loot because the particular shopkeeper whose merchandise is accessible may give him a part-time job this summer. This student is operating at the Stage Two "Self-Benefit" level. Another student (at Stage Three) might be afraid that others will look down on him for stealing, while another (at Stage Four) believes that people in general will not have safe, orderly lives if individuals take advantage of social turmoil by such activities as looting. All of these students have chosen not to loot, but the reasons, not the action, decide their placement at four different levels.

To use the sample dilemmas for developing moral reasoning at more advanced levels, the teacher needs to work sequentially. On the basis of some experimentation with students, Kohlberg concluded that students can understand stages of moral reasoning below their own and possibly one stage above their own. But the students he worked with (asking them to read moral reasoning statements and then state them in their own words) were almost never able to understand two or more stages above their own level.

It follows that teachers might be able to lead students to consider the level above their dominant level, but students will probably become confused if they are asked to understand levels much more advanced. On the basis of the teacher's diagnosis of the student's dominant level, the teacher can probe for thinking at the next stage.

Teachers are reminded that their role is to help the student think rather than to tell him or her what to think. So the teacher would never criticize a student for low-level reasoning and demand that he or she reason on a higher level. Instead, the teacher would lead the student by careful questioning to consideration of alternatives. The emphasis is on inner growth and change and not on outward conformity.

Employing the dilemmas as a means toward growth, the teacher will work within the bounds of the students' maturity and maturational levels. For example, it would not be realistic to expect a young student who does not yet think on an abstract level to respond to a dilemma in terms of systems of laws or principles of justice. Again, the emphasis is on growth one level at a time as the individual moves from childhood, through adolescence to adulthood.

Needless to say, no teacher at a single grade level would set himself or herself the goal of moving students through all six stages. That is the task of a lifetime. Instead, the teacher tries to prevent stagnation or fixation at a given level. As long as there is movement and it is at a natural, integrated pace, the teacher is succeeding.

HOW TO DO IT

Some specific tips for exploring the dilemmas may help teachers make maximum diagnostic and growth use of them. The following procedures should help assure effective discussion:

1. Present the dilemma clearly to the students so that all terms and words are understood.

2. Have students state the dilemma in their own words. It is often helpful to write the dilemma statement on the board.

3. Phrase questions to promote discussion. "Why" and "How" questions are preferable to those answerable by a "yes" or "no."

4. When students ask questions, except those for clarification of directions, refer the questions to the group.

5. Re-phrase questions if answers are not promptly given.

6. Summarize comments frequently. Involve less verbal students by asking them to summarize if they will be able to do so.

7. Try to find value in each serious comment. If it seems off the topic, ask the contributor to explain how it relates.

8. Identify the differences among the positions expressed by group members.

9. Allow sufficient time to explore the subject. Encourage alternative considerations.

The teacher is encouraged to employ the teaching strategies described in Chapter 5. Dilemmas should frequently be role-played to allow students to experiment at the feeling and involvement level with the solution they have chosen. The "Fish Bowl" is a framework which focuses discussion and assures participation. A simulation might be developed by expanding the material of a given dilemma. The teacher should use a variety of techniques to explore dilemmas affectively, cognitively and through psycho-motor activity. Variety will also contribute to a high level of interest.

8

Dilemmas
For The Classroom

These dilemmas are presented in three sections: (1) Primary, (2) Elementary, and (3) Junior and Senior High School. But teachers are the best judge of the maturity of their students; so teachers should decide which dilemmas seem appropriate for their classes.

Dilemmas begin with a broad *Objective* which defines the area of moral reasoning. It is followed by the *Situation* which is the dilemma story. The *Focus* question is the choice for students to consider. The *Discussion* section begins with the crucial "Explain your decision." (Remember that in order to determine the level of moral reasoning and to guide the student to the next higher level, the teacher will need to understand the student's *reasons* for the choice he or she makes.)

If lively discussion follows the focus and explanation questions, the teacher may not need to use the discussion questions. (They may arise naturally in the course of the students' discussion.) Discussion questions are best used to retrieve a straying discussion or to "prime" students if ideas are not flowing.

The dilemmas move from simple to complex as they move from primary to the high school level. A "right" answer to some of the simpler dilemmas might seem apparent to the teacher, but to a very young student, the situation may not be clear cut at all. It is important to build an atmosphere in which students who can guess the teacher's response to the dilemma will not compliantly offer up that response. Such an atmosphere may develop slowly because students are experienced at telling teachers what they want to hear. Teachers might want to arrange the order of the dilemmas so that students' first contact will be with ones where the "adult" answer would not be apparent. Then, as trust develops, students will be able to give their own answers even when they know they might conflict with the teacher's.

The situation, the focus question and the discussion questions are all written in language that might be used with students. Informality is desirable; the teacher is encouraged to use his or her own words to make the situations seem as real as possible.

The dilemmas presented here are points of departure. Teachers should adapt, revise, expand upon them as they see fit. In fact, some of the best dilemmas are those students and teachers write together out of real-life situations. (Chapter 9 offers some pointers for creating such dilemmas.) The following dilemmas are suggestions and beginnings. Teachers are urged to be creative!

Dilemma No. 1 — Primary Level

SHOULD I TELL?

OBJECTIVE:

You see a group of older boys taking money from younger ones on your way home from school. They tell you not to report them or they will beat you up. You feel bad, but go home. You are upset and don't eat dinner. Your mother asks what is wrong.

FOCUS:

Do you tell your mother?

DISCUSSION: 1

1. Explain your decision.

2. What will happen if you tell your mother?

3. What if you don't?

4. Will the older boys try to steal from you?

Dilemma No. 2 — Primary Level

THE CAT IN THE TREE

OBJECTIVE:

To explore a conflict between following the rules and helping another person.

SITUATION:

On your way to school you see a kindergartner crying because his cat is stuck in a tree. You would like to climb the tree and get the cat, but you will be late for school if you do. Still, you hate to leave the little boy crying when you could help him.

FOCUS:

Do you help the boy and arrive late for school?

DISCUSSION:

1. Explain your decision.

2. What will happen if you don't help the child?

3. What will happen if you are late for school?

4. Will your teacher accept your reason for being late.?

5. Would you change your mind if you knew your teacher would tell your parents you were late?

Dilemma No. 3 — Primary Level

A GIFT FOR YOUR BEST FRIEND

OBJECTIVE:

To examine friendship and sharing.

SITUATION:

It's your best friend's birthday. You have saved five dollars to buy him a nice gift. When you go to the store to buy the present you see a model kit you've wanted for ages. You are tempted to buy yourself the model and get your friend a smaller gift.

FOCUS:

Do you buy yourself the model and get your friend a smaller gift?

DISCUSSION:

1. Explain your decision.

2. Would you rather buy for others or for yourself?

3. Will your friend care what gift he receives?

4. Will you feel differently giving your friend a smaller or larger gift?

Dilemma No. 4 — Primary Level

HOW DID KATHY GET HURT?

OBJECTIVE:

To examine truthfulness when it implicates a friend.

SITUATION:

You are working at your desk. You look up to see Mary pull the chair from under Kathy. Kathy appears to be hurt. The teacher asks for information about how she was hurt. The teacher asks if anyone can tell what happened. Both girls are your friends.

FOCUS:

Do you tell or do you remain silent?

DISCUSSION:

1. Explain your decision.

2. What if Kathy is hurt badly and taken to the hospital? Does this change your mind?

3. How do you feel about the friend who has done this?

4. Is she still your friend?

5. How would you feel if she did this to you?

6.   What will happen if you tell the teacher what you saw?

7.   Will Mary be your friend if you tell on her?

Dilemma No. 5 — Primary Level

THE STORMY DAY

OBJECTIVE:

To examine trust.

SITUATION:

Your parents have told you never to get in a car with anyone but them. It is a stormy day and your friend's parents, whom you have never met, offer to take you home. Your friend is in the car. You want to go with them because you are cold and wet. It is ten blocks to your home!

FOCUS:

Do you accept a ride?

DISCUSSION:

1. Explain your decision.

2. Do you trust your friend's parents?

3. Does this make a difference?

4. What if you arrive home and your parents see you leave the car?

5. Could you explain that it was "safe" to do this?

6. Should you use your own judgment or follow their rule?

Dilemma No. 6 — Primary Level

GRANDFATHER'S WATCH

OBJECTIVE:

To examine whether to tell the truth even when it may bring retaliation.

SITUATION:

Your grandfather and grandmother have come to visit for the weekend. One of grandfather's most prized possessions is a gold watch which was given to him by his father. Although you have been told not to enter the guest room, you and your sister go in to look at the watch.

Just then, Grandmother calls, "Girls, where are you?" Your sister is so startled that she accidentally drops the watch. Your sister says if you tell on her she'll tell about the trouble you were in last week at school.

FOCUS:

Do you tell?

DISCUSSION:

1.   Explain your decision.

2.   Should you tell Grandmother that both of you are responsible?

3.   Does it make a difference that you didn't touch the watch?

Dilemma No. 7 — Primary Level

PET DAY AT SCHOOL

OBJECTIVE:

To examine honesty when it may cause unpleasant consequences.

SITUATION:

During recess, Jim and Don enter the room laughing. They do not know that you are in the back of the room.

Your teacher allows each student to bring a pet one day during the school year. Today students have brought a rabbit, a frog and a goldfish. The boys stand by the animals, whispering and laughing. Then they leave the room.

You see the boys have poured pencil shavings over the goldfish and glue on the frog. You grab the goldfish bowl and run for the sink. Just as you get the goldfish into another bowl the class enters and discovers the frog covered with glue. Your teacher walks toward the animals and shoots a disapproving glance at you.

You begin to explain and see Jim and Don with angry looks on their faces. They realize that you must have seen them.

FOCUS:

Do you tell your teacher the other boys played the prank?

DISCUSSION:

1.   Explain your decision.

2.   What will happen if you do not tell?

3.   Will the class think you hurt the animals?

4.   How do you think the other boys will treat you if you tell?

5.   How would you feel if you had done something wrong and someone told on you?

Dilemma No. 8 — Primary Level

MOTHER'S VISIT

OBJECTIVE:

To examine how you react to the judgments of others.

SITUATION:

There have been problems with some children throwing food in the school cafeteria. Last week it was so bad that the principal had to call the parents of misbehaving children. The parents had to come to school and eat with their children.

Today as you reach your cafeteria table, you see your mother sitting there. She's come to surprise you by eating with the class. It's a nice surprise, but the other students won't understand that your mother is here as a guest. They'll believe the principal had to call your mother.

Your mother made a special effort to get here from work just to eat with you. But students from the other table are anxious to find out who is going to sit by your mother.

FOCUS:

What do you do?

DISCUSSION:

1. Explain your decision.

2. Can you explain to your mother?

3. To the other children?

4. What if you left and went out on the playground instead of eating lunch?

Dilemma No. 9 — Elementary Level

LITTLE SISTER

OBJECTIVE:

To examine the issues of responsibility and loyalty.

SITUATION:

It's Halloween night. You agree to take your younger sister out to "Trick or Treat."

As you leave your house you see several friends approaching from the opposite side of the street. You join them, although they are not very happy to have Angie along. Tommy suggests that everyone take a scary short cut across a vacant lot and down several dark alleys. Your sister is frightened and begins to cry.

You want to go with the rest of your gang. Your sister can go home by herself if she listens carefully to your directions.

FOCUS:

Do you let your sister go home alone?

DISCUSSION:

1. Explain your decision.

2. What is your responsibility for Angie?

3. When did you accept it?

4.   If you agree to do something, must you follow through?

5.   Or does your obligation change when circumstances change?

6.   What difference would it make if your friends said they were tired of playing with you because Angie always got in the way?

Dilemma No. 10 — Elementary Levsl

THE CLASS BULLY

OBJECTIVE:

To practice decision-making.

SITUATION:

You are with a group of friends on the playground at recess. The class bully has just called you a "dirty" name. Your friends urge you to fight. You know that in a fair fight, the bully will win. Yet you do not want your friends to think you are "chicken."

FOCUS:

Do you fight the bully?

DISCUSSION:

1. Explain your decision.

2. What are the choices you have?

3. Is fighting acceptable if you have been insulted?

4. Would you fight if you thought you could win?

5. Would your friends fight the bully if the same thing happened to them?

6. Would your decision be different if you knew that you would be sent to the principal's office if you get into a fight?

Dilemma No. 11 — Elementary Level

THE MATH TEST

OBJECTIVE:

To promote honesty and responsibility.

SITUATION:

Your best friend cheated on a math test. You know this because she told you, and you saw her get the answers from the boy next to her. You also know that this test is important in the final grading, and that you and your friend are the closest competition for the top honor in scholarship.

FOCUS:

Do you try to stop the cheating?

DISCUSSION:

1. Explain your decision.

2. Is it your responsibility to tell the teacher?

3. Do you talk to your friend?

4. Do you consider it none of your business?

5. How do you feel if you do nothing and your friend continues to cheat?

6. What if she gets higher grades than you?

7.   Would it make any difference if she were not your best friend?

8.   What difference would it make if neither of you were close to a scholarship honor?

Dilemma No. 12 — Elementary Level

PATROL DUTY

OBJECTIVE:

To explore responsibility and the consequences.

SITUATION:

You patrol a crosswalk near school. Every morning older students come by to tease and threaten you. You know if you tell your teacher, the older students will find out you told. Then you'll really be in trouble.

FOCUS:

What do you do?

DISCUSSION:

1. Explain your decision.

2. Can you make the older students understand your job as a patrol?

3. Can you seek help from anyone?

4. How can you protect yourself?

Dilemma No. 13 — Elementary Level

THE PLAYGROUND FIGHT

OBJECTIVE:

To examine integrity and responsibility.

SITUATION:

You have been wrongly accused of fighting on the playground. Your teacher tells you to go to the office to see the principal. You've been in fights before so you're sure the principal won't believe you're innocent. You notice that it is just five minutes until the end of school. You are tempted to sneak out the back door and go home since you know you weren't in the fight anyway.

FOCUS:

Do you stay and see the principal?

DISCUSSION:

1. Explain your decision.

2. What will happen if you go home?

3. Does the fact that you are innocent (and your teacher is wrong) give you the right to disobey your teacher's orders?

Dilemma No. 14 — Elementary Level

RUNNING THE STOP SIGN

OBJECTIVE:

To explore justice.

SITUATION:

Your older sister just received her driver's license. She asks your parents for the car to go shopping. She takes you with her. On the way home, she runs a stop sign. You tell your parents, and they restrict her from using the car for two weeks.

During that time your mother takes you to the store and she runs a stop sign. When you remind her that your sister was restricted for the same thing, you are punished for being sassy. You think the punishment - no T.V. for a week - is unfair.

FOCUS:

Since you feel it is an unfair punishment, do you watch T.V. anyway?

DISCUSSION:

1.   Explain your decision.

2.   Can you talk with your mother and change her mind about punishing you?

3.   Do you tell your sister about what happened?

4. Should you ask your father to talk with your mother about it?

5. Should you get permission to go to a friend's house to study, but watch your favorite T.V. show instead?

Dilemma No. 15 — Elementary Level

THE POOL PASS

OBJECTIVE:

To explore honesty and respect.

SITUATION:

Your mother and father have weekend guests. Your sister is away for the weekend. Your parents want you to use your sister's pool pass for their guests' daughter. They tell you to take her to the pool for the afternoon, reminding you to be sure you call her by your sister's name. You think this is wrong, yet your parents have told you to do this. The guest is asking you to "hurry-up."

FOCUS:

Do you go ahead and do as you are told?

DISCUSSION:

1. Explain your decision.

2. Should go you go ahead because your parents have told you to do it?

3. Who is responsible?

4. Is it right to disobey your parents in this situation?

5.   What will you do if a friend of yours sees
that the guest is not your sister, but hears you call
her by your sister's name?

Dilemma No. 16 — Elementary Level

MAKING CHANGE

OBJECTIVE:

To examine honesty and respect.

SITUATION:

Your parents have always told you to be honest. Yesterday you saw your dad receive too much change for a purchase. He said nothing about it until he was out of the store. Then he bragged about receiving $20.00 change for a $10.00 bill. Today, in the cafeteria line at school, you receive too much change for the dollar you gave the cashier.

FOCUS:

Do you tell the cashier about the error?

DISCUSSION:

1. Explain your decision.

2. Did your dad do the right thing in keeping the money?

3. Should you follow your dad's example?

4. Do you talk this over with your parents?

5. What if your friend who is behind you in line will think you're crazy if you tell the cashier?

6. Is it the cashier's problem and not yours?

Dilemma No. 17 — Elementary Level

THE FIVE-DOLLAR BILL

OBJECTIVE:

To examine undeserved praise and personal integrity.

SITUATION:

At school you and your friends find a five-dollar bill in the hallway. Your friends decide to turn the money in to the school office. You argue that you should all spend the money, but they won't listen. The principal praises all of you for turning in the money . . . he had lost it out of his pocket and had been looking for it.

FOCUS:

Do you accept the praise?

DISCUSSION:

1. Explain your decision.

2. If you accept the praise, how will you feel?

3. What will your friends think of you?

4. What else could you do?

5. Does it make any difference who had lost the money?

6. What if it were part of a special school fund for buying a new flag?

Dilemma No. 18 — Elementary Level

CANDY FOR A VOTE

OBJECTIVE:

To explore the value of fair play.

SITUATION:

A fifth grade student is running for president of the school. Everything you know about this student is good. During the campaign the student comes to you and offers you a candy bar if you vote for her.

FOCUS:

Do you object to this way of trying to win?

DISCUSSION:

1. Explain your decision.

2. Do you vote for the candidate?

3. Are these tactics wrong?

4. Will she win the election unless someone tells an authority what she is doing?

5. Is this fair to the other candidate?

6. Is it any business of yours?

Dilemma No. 19 — Elementary Level

THE LOST DOLLAR

OBJECTIVE:

To discuss the effects of prejudice.

SITUATION:

Billy is a new boy at school. He is an Indian. Today some of the boys in class accused him of taking your dollar. You thought you put the dollar in your jacket pocket. The other boys said Billy probably took it because all Indians steal. You accuse Billy of stealing your money.

Then you see your dollar bill on the floor — it must have fallen out of your pocket. You feel too ashamed to say anything to Billy or to the other boys so you stuff it quickly into your pocket.

FOCUS:

Do you make it right with Billy?

DISCUSSION:

1. Explain your decision.

2. Do you apologize to Billy and tell the other boys you found your money?

3. Why were the students so quick to blame Billy?

4. What is prejudice?

5. Could the teacher have helped in this situation? How?

6. What if Billy saw you stuff the dollar bill into your pocket? Does this make a difference?

Dilemma No. 20 — Elementary Level

THE MONEY ON THE COUNTER

OBJECTIVE:

To discuss the limits of loyalty.

SITUATION:

You are with a group of friends in the corner grocery store. Your friend finds a ten-dollar bill on the counter. While you wait for the clerk to total your purchases, a woman enters the store. She is very upset. She tells the clerk she has lost a ten-dollar bill and thinks she may have left it in the store. She and the clerk begin a search for the money. Your friend makes a sign for you to keep quiet.

FOCUS:

Do you tell the woman your friend found the money?

DISCUSSION:

1. Explain your decision.

2. If you tell the clerk your friend has the money, will he still be your friend?

3. If you don't tell the clerk, what are the possible effects for the woman who lost the money?

4.   What if you were the one who lost the ten-dollar bill?

Dilemma No. 21 — Elementary Level

WASTEBASKET ON FIRE!

OBJECTIVE:

To explore responsibility for actions of others.

SITUATION:

Your school has been vandalized frequently during the last month. Windows have been broken repeatedly, painted letters and words have been written on the walls. The principal has requested that each student help by reporting anyone seen destroying property. The principal explained that your parents pay taxes to maintain the schools.

You observe one of your friends setting fire to a wastebasket.

FOCUS:

Do you report your friend to the principal?

DISCUSSION:

1. Explain your decision.

2. Should you protect your friend in all cases?

3. What might happen if you don't report the incident?

4. What if the person you observed is not your friend? Does this make a difference?

Dilemma No. 22 — Elementary Level

THE YAHTZEE GAME

OBJECTIVE:

To explore some of the consequences of dishonesty.

SITUATION:

One evening you play Yahtzee with your best friend. He has won the last five games. It's your turn. You roll, but the fifth die falls off the table onto the floor. Your friend is adding his score and doesn't see your roll. You can move the die to get the score you need.

FOCUS:

Do you cheat?

DISCUSSION:

1. Explain your decision.

2. Will you be happy winning if you cheat?

3. Does it matter that this is just a game and does not effect anyone else?

4. How would you feel if your friend cheated you?

5. Is there any other way you could win?

6. Why do you need to win?

Dilemma No. 23 — Elementary Level

TEASING TOMMY

OBJECTIVE:

To clarify the values of justice and kindness.

SITUATION:

As you approach the playground you hear the students teasing Tommy about being fat. Tommy is in the center of a circle with his eyes closed and tears streaming down his face.

Earlier in the year you defended another student and no one talked to you for three days. You hesitate.

FOCUS:

Do you help Tommy?

DISCUSSION:

1. Explain your decision.

2. Can you be nice to Tommy later when no one is looking?

3. Do you need friends more than Tommy needs protection?

4. Would it make a difference if Tommy had teased you last week?

Dilemma No. 24 — Elementary Level

THE BOX OF CANDY

OBJECTIVE:

To determine when actions indicate selfishness.

SITUATION:

You are a new fifth grader at school. You listen attentively as your teacher describes the prize given for the best social studies project. Later you find that the prize is a box of candy.

You work hard on your project. Soon the big day arrives. Your teacher chooses your project for the prize.

You are anxious to show the prize to your parents. You watch the candy sitting on your desk until the dismissal bell rings. As you race for the door a loud voice behind you says, "What a stingy guy! He wouldn't even share his candy with the rest of us!"

FOCUS:

What do you do?

DISCUSSION:

1. Explain your decision.

2. Do the other students have the right to expect some candy?

3. Do you have the right to want your parents to share your happiness in winning and see the unopened box of candy?

4. Who is selfish, you, or the other students?

5. Is there any way you could explain to the other students how you feel?

6. Would sharing the candy help make friends?

DILEMMA No. 25 — Elementary Level

BUYING THE BOAT

OBJECTIVE:

To examine cheating

SITUATION:

You and two friends regularly play on a friend's rowboat. You fish, row out to the middle of the lake and swim, or just row across the lake and talk. Last week you found that the boat is for sale. You and your friends decide to buy the boat together. The other two boys have the money. You are ten dollars short.

You go to your father's grocery store after the discussion. Your father asks you to tend the store while he works in the stockroom.

Rich old Mr. Kelly, one of dad's best customers, enters the store. Mr. Kelly's eyesight has been failing him. You help the old man pick out several things and brings them to the counter for check out. The bill is $9.53. Mr. Kelly hands you a bill and says, "I can't believe the prices these days. A few pennies is all you get back from a ten-dollar bill." Mr. Kelly makes a mistake and gives you a twenty-dollar bill. You can keep the extra ten dollars and buy the boat you want. Mr. Kelly believes he is giving you ten dollars and your dad is not losing money.

FOCUS:

Do you keep the ten dollars?

DISCUSSION:

1. Explain your decision.

2. What are some possible consequences if you keep the money?

3. Would you feel guilty enjoying the boat?

4. What if Mr. Kelly finds out he gave you a twenty-dollar bill?

5. Shouldn't Mr. Kelly share his wealth anyway?

6. Does he have a right to so much when all you want is a little rowboat?

7. What do you think about taking the money now and paying him back secretly when you can?

Dilemma No. 26 — Elementary Level

BIKE MONEY

OBJECTIVE:

To examine a conflict between personal wishes and family responsibilities.

SITUATION:

You have been saving money from your paper route for over a year to purchase a bicycle. Another eleven dollars and you will have the purchase price. Your father was laid-off from his job a month ago. The family's budget is tight. Next week you will have the additional money required to purchase the bike. But your family could use the money to pay bills and buy food.

FOCUS:

Do you buy the bicycle?

DISCUSSION:

1. Explain your decision.

2. What are the alternatives in this situation?

3. Can you reach a compromise?

4. How do you decide if your wishes or your family's needs come first?

Dilemma No. 27 — Jr. High and High School

THE SCIENCE TEST

OBJECTIVE:

To examine solutions when unfairly judged.

SITUATION:

You are taking an important science test. You have studied for several days and you feel confident that you will be able to make a good grade.

As your science teacher passes out the test, he says that if he sees anyone talking, that person will fail the test.

When you receive your test you get right to work. The girl next to you asks for help on a question. You motion to her that she is not to talk, and that you will not help her out. Your science teacher sees you and tears up your test.

You feel terrible, even close to tears! The girl explains to the science teacher that she was asking for your help. The science teacher says he did not see her talking. The girl tears up her test paper, saying she was the one at fault. She demands that she receive a failure for her test. The science teacher refuses. Everyone in the class thinks the teacher was unfair.

FOCUS:

What do you do?

DISCUSSION:

1. Explain your decision.

2. Think of several things you could do — which one is best?

3. Can anyone help you solve the problem?

4. What will your parents think when they learn that you failed the test?

5. How should you react to unfair actions from others?

Dilemma No. 28 — Jr. High and High School

TV "NEWS"

OBJECTIVE:

To examine honesty in business practices.

SITUATION:

You are a member of a TV camera crew sent to film a college campus disturbance. When you arrive the young people are milling around quietly. Most of them are leaving the area where the confrontation took place.

The film director is disappointed. He suggests that you talk to the leaders to stir up anger and hostility again. If this occurs the director could get some excellent film for television. He is waiting for you to act on his suggestion.

FOCUS:

Do you attempt to incite a disturbance?

DISCUSSION:

1. Explain your decision.

2. What might happen if you do as the director wishes?

3. What are the possible results if you refuse to do it?

4. Will your TV viewers have a false impression of the disturbance?

5. What if you are being considered for assistant film director? Does this make a difference in your decision?

Dilemma No. 29 — Jr. High and High School

HIKE FOR HUNGER

OBJECTIVE:

To solve a conflict between telling the truth and fulfilling one's promises.

SITUATION:

You are a participant in the Hike for Hunger — a 25-mile march to help feed the hungry people of the world. Your sponsors have agreed to pay to the relief fund an amount ranging from $.25 to $2.00 for each mile you walk.

On the day of the march you meet your friend Tom. You agree together that you will walk the entire 25 miles. After ten miles Tom collapses from heat exhaustion and is taken to the first aid station. You have no other friends among the marchers. After 20 miles your feet are numb and you ache all over. The relief truck pulls up and the driver asks if anyone wants to quit. Several people climb aboard and the driver punches their cards to show how far they walked. Just as the truck pulls away, you climb aboard. The driver doesn't know you are there and the other people are too tired to care. You sit quietly and do not talk with anyone.

FOCUS:

Do you tell the driver you quit at 20 miles or claim the entire 25 miles?

DISCUSSION:

1. Explain your decision.

2. Does the fact that proceeds go to charity affect your choice?

3. If you claim 25 miles, more money will go to feed the hungry. What difference will it make to your sponsors?

4. No one will know if you claim 25 miles. Does this make a difference in your decision?

Dilemma No. 30 — Jr High and High School

THE SHOPPING TRIP

OBJECTIVE:

To explore reactions to a windfall that is not honestly yours.

SITUATION:

You are the mother of an active family and have just completed the weekly grocery shopping. It costs so much to feed your family basic meals that there is no money for treats and surprises for the children. You are dwelling on this thought as you reach the parcel pick-up area.

The boy who normally loads the groceries is not there but his substitute comes out of the store in a few moments. He loads the groceries and you drive away.

You arrive home, unload the groceries and are immediately aware that this is not your order. It is filled with high priced items — steaks, roasts and extras you could not afford.

FOCUS:

Do you return the food?

DISCUSSION:

1. Explain your decision.

2. If you keep the groceries, how will you explain to your family?

3. Is it dishonest to keep the groceries?

4. Does your family deserve to "share the wealth" with whoever purchased the groceries?

5. Have the profits the store makes from your regular shopping entitled you to this "bonus"?

Dilemma No. 31 — Jr. High and High School

TREE GROWING

OBJECTIVE:

To solve a conflict between justice and friendship.

SITUATION:

The student cooperative association at your school has purchased special trees for the school. Students worked to raise the money. You attend the assembly the day the trees are planted and share the feeling of accomplishment. Several weeks later you pass the school and you see several cars parked near the front of the school. Loud laughing and conversation can be heard. You see the cars drive over the curb and head for the newly planted trees. The first car rides over a tree, snapping it in half. You feel sick with disgust and walk faster toward your home. As you turn the corner the cars pass you. You recognize one of the drivers. It is your friend's older brother.

FOCUS:

Do you report his actions?

DISCUSSION:

1. Explain your decision.

2.   Do you feel you have a responsibility to report what you know?

3.   How would your reporting affect your friendship?

4.   What if other passersby saw the cars drive away, and you think they will report what they saw and heard? Does this make a difference in your decision?

5.   Would it make a difference if your identity could be kept secret?

Dilemma No. 32 — Jr. High and High School

DRESS CODE

OBJECTIVE:

To examine a conflict between individual freedom and community standards.

SITUATION:

Most teachers wear jeans and sweatshirts to school. Since this trend began, the discipline in the school has deteriorated. Students are wearing even more casual clothes — bare midriffs, very short pants, tank tops, backless and transparent blouses. Some have arrived without shoes. Both students and staff believe that the authorities have no right to dictate a code of personal dress or grooming.

You are the school principal. Some parents believe that the situation is outrageous and should be corrected immediately. They are ready to ask for your dismissal on the grounds that you have not exercised leadership. They claim both students and staff are out of control.

FOCUS:

Do you prescribe a dress code?

DISCUSSION:

1. Explain your decision.

2. Is it possible to compromise in this situation?

3. Do we infringe on an individuals' rights if we require him or her to adhere to a basic code of dress?

4. Who should make the final decision?

5. When you are under pressure from two sides, do you side with those who press hardest?

6. Do you save your job at any cost, then work at making changes you feel are right on a gradual basis?

Dilemma No. 33 — Jr. High and High School

AUNT WILMA

OBJECTIVE:

To explore the responsibilities of family life and loyalty in family relationships.

SITUATION:

You have lived in a small town for six months. You are excitedly planning your sixteenth birthday party. It will be the first time you have had your new friends over, and you hope it will make you a permanent member of their group at school. You want very much to be a part of the group.

On the day of the party you and your mother make preparations. You put the finishing touches on the buffet tables and get dressed for the party.

As you come downstairs you hear your mother talking, and someone laughing loudly. Your heart sinks! It's your Aunt Wilma. You think (and so does your mother) that she's outlandish. She tries to be the life of every party, and admires you to the point of embarrassment.

You know she will embarrass you in front of your guests. You are afraid this will ruin your chances with the group. But she loves you very much and will be devastated if you ask her to leave.

FOCUS:

What do you do?

DISCUSSION:

1. Explain your decision.

2. How do you act in this situation?

3. Who can help you?

4. What are the alternatives?

5. How will your friends react in each solution?

6. What is your first responsibility?

Dilemma No. 34 — Jr. High and High School

PLAYBOY PICTURE

OBJECTIVE:

To examine whether a need for money justifies a compromise in values.

SITUATION:

You need money badly to go to college. College is your ambition, and your parents' ambition for you. They would like to help you, but they do not earn enough money.

You receive an offer to model for *Playboy* magazine. From a single nude picture you could earn enough for a year at the university of your choice.

FOCUS:

Do you make the picture?

DISCUSSION:

1. Explain your decision.

2. Do you feel you would compromise your values by making the picture?

3. What are the issues in this situation?

4. What if you decide not to model for *Playboy*?

5.   How else can you obtain funds for your college education?

6.   What if your parents are shown the center-fold? How do you justify it to them?

7.   If you cannot afford college you will not become a nurse and benefit humanity. Is the good you can do with a college education more important than the disadvantages of making the picture?

Dilemma No. 35 — Jr. High and High School

RE-ELECTION CAMPAIGN

OBJECTIVE:

To use problem-solving skills in situations involving honesty.

SITUATION:

You are a politician campaigning for re-election. Your record indicates that you have been honest in your voting record and representation of the voters in your district. This election is the closest race of your career, and you have been invited to share a political ticket with two candidates whose reputation for honesty is doubtful. Many of their actions and decisions have not been made in the best interests of the voters. Yet they are backed by a powerful political organization able to almost guarantee your re-election.

FOCUS:

Do you accept their offer to join forces?

DISCUSSION:

1. Explain your decision.

2. If you join with them will the voters lose faith in you?

3. Since you know you are honest does it matter if the other two candidates have dubious reputations?

4. What are the implications of your name appearing on the same ballot with theirs?

5. Can you accept the offer and not be indebted to them for favors and special privileges?

6. Is winning the first priority?

Dilemma No. 36 — Jr. High and High School

DEVELOPMENT PLANNING

OBJECTIVE:

To explore the attitudes needed to cope with change.

SITUATION:

You are a member of the city council, and it has been suggested that you take the lead in preparing an important development planning measure. Unplanned development in your city is devastating wildlife and overloading the water and sewage systems. It is predicted that open land will be gone by 1990. Several citizen groups urge laws limiting growth of the city.

The influential businessmen of the city are opposed to any legislation that would stop development. You are up for re-election in six months and these businessmen usually contribute considerable money to your campaign.

FOCUS:

What do you do?

DISCUSSION:

1. Explain your decision.

2.   Is change inevitable?

3.   Could someone else sponsor the bill so that it would not be tied to you?

4.   Can you offer the businessmen a compromise for their support of the measure?

5.   What is your first responsibility?

6.   Should you sponsor the measure in the interest of public welfare?

7.   Would it make any difference in your decision if you owned some land which was suitable both for residential housing or a park area?

Dilemma No. 37 — Jr. High and High School

COMMERCIAL ARTIST

OBJECTIVE:

To explore a conflict between loyalty and self-fulfillment.

SITUATION:

You are nineteen years old. More than anything else you want to be a commercial artist. You have done well in art in school and have an art job promised by a friend. Your father, however, wants you to be a businessman like himself. You argue and you leave in a gloomy mood.

You visit an old friend for advice. He tells you that "each man must choose his own way." You know the words are true but in all your life you have never disobeyed your father's wishes. If you are to take the art job you must leave home immediately to work in a commercial art studio in a city about a hundred miles away.

FOCUS:

Do you follow your father's wishes?

DISCUSSION:

1. Explain your decision.

2.   Who should make the final decision?

3.   What are the factors that influence your decision?

4.   What is the most important issue in this choice?

Dilemma No. 38 — Jr. High and High School

THE PLASTIC BAG

OBJECTIVE:

To explore loyalty and friendship.

SITUATION:

You and your friend are walking to your home after school. He asks you to take care of his books and a plastic bag overnight. He says he plans to use the plastic bag for a science experiment tomorrow. You agree, take his things and go home.

That evening, your mother comes to your room demanding to know here you got the bag of marijuana, and if you've used any of it.

You tell her you didn't know what it was, and are just keeping it overnight for a friend. Your mother thinks this is a flimsy story. She asks who the friend is, where he got it, what you did with him, etc., etc., etc.

You know your mother will tell your friend's mother, but she won't believe you unless you reveal his name.

FOCUS:

Do you tell your mother who your friend is?

DISCUSSION:

    1. Explain your decision.

    2. Did your friend know it was marijuana?

    3. If you tell, what will happen to your friend?

    4. Is loyalty to your friend the main issue?

Dilemma No. 39 — Jr. High and High School

THE WHIZ-KID PILL

OBJECTIVE:

To examine responsibility for others.

SITUATION:

You are a teacher in the year 2000. A new pill is available that allows students to learn faster for short periods of time. It has been tested on animals and appears to have no adverse effects.

You have access to the medication. You can use it on the slow learners in your class. You can secure permission from the children's parents because you have a good reputation and parents trust your judgment. This pill will change the children's natural brain functions and response patterns. It will increase their ability to learn for a short period.

FOCUS:

Do you use the pill in your class?

DISCUSSION:

1. Explain your decision.

2. Would you be violating the students'
rights by deciding by yourself which ones would
get the pill?

3. What effect would this medication have
on your relationship with students to whom the
pill was given? With the other students?

4. Would it be fair to give the pill to only a
few selected students? Which ones ?

Dilemma No. 40 — Jr. High and High School

MEDICAL AUTOPSY

OBJECTIVE:

To think critically in situations involving human relationships.

SITUATION:

Your closest relative just died from a rare disease. Little is known about the symptoms or the treatment of the disease. The doctor has requested permission to perform an autopsy to reveal how effective the new medicine proved against the disease and to verify the cause of death. He tells you that the knowledge might help cure someone else suffering from the illness. You are sure that the autopsy would not have been the wish of your relative.

FOCUS:

Do you agree to the autopsy?

DISCUSSION:

1.   Explain your decision.

2.   Do you have any responsibility to your relativ in this decision?

3.   What issues should be considered?

4.   ould the religious beliefs of the deceased make a difference?

5.   Is the good of the living the first priority?

Dilemma No. 41 — Jr. High and High School

REPORT CARD DAY

OBJECTIVE:

To examine honesty and responsibility.

SITUATION:

You are on your way home from school with your report card. You wonder if this report will be better than the previous ones. Your marks have never been very good.

On weekends you help your father at the filling station, and on Saturdays you have learned to tune engines so well that they almost purr. Cars fascinate you.

Now that you are outside you open the envelope. The marks are mostly D's. You know that your parents are so busy they might not notice if you fail to bring home the report card. You know how to sign your father's name perfectly. If you show your parents this report card it will mean no more work at the filling station. You will have to study even on weekends. You think it makes good sense to develop your skill with cars.

FOCUS:

Do you show your parents the report card?

DISCUSSION:

1. Explain your decision.

2. What are the alternatives?

3. What are the advantages and disadvantages of the solution you chose?

4. What will be your parents reaction in each solution?

5. What decision will serve you best in the long run?

6. How can you best be true to yourself?

Dilemma No. 42 — Jr. High and High School Level

CONSTRUCTION CONTRACTOR

OBJECTIVE:

To consider priorities in responsibility.

SITUATION:

You are manager and part-owner of a young, growing construction company. Your firm has been awarded the contract to build a new Community Center. You have been negotiating with the city for months. If you complete the project according to schedule, other large contracts will be given to you.

Near the construction site are several old houses. The historical society plans to restore them later this year. The houses block easy access to a main road and will slow down construction work. You could move materials much quicker if they were not there.

You find a provision in your contract which would let you demolish the old houses.

FOCUS:

Do you demolish the old houses?

DISCUSSION:

1. Explain your decision.

2. What is your first responsibility?

3. Is getting your job done efficiently the prime consideration?

4. What are some alternatives?

Dilemma No. 43 — Jr. High and High School

MARRIAGE OR CAREER?

OBJECTIVE:

To examine a possible conflict between marriage and career.

SITUATION:

You have recently graduated from high school. You and your boyfriend hope to be married this year. Your parents urge you to wait. You have always wanted to go to art school, and your high school art teachers say you have real talent. If you marry, you will need to work for a few years at least. It may be difficult to go back to school.

FOCUS:

Do you marry?

DISCUSSION:

1.   Explain your decision.

2.   Do you think you will be happy with your choice five years from now?

3.   Describe some possible consequences of your choice?

4.   Who can help you reach a solution?

Dilemma No. 44 — Jr. High and High School

THE VISITING FRIEND

OBJECTIVE:

To explore a conflict of loyalties.

SITUATION:

A close friend moves to another state. After two years he comes to visit. He has changed a lot, both in the way he talks and the way he acts. You know he is using drugs in the house because he has asked you to join him. Your parents would be upset to know what he is doing and would probably inform his parents. Your friend says he knows what he is doing.

FOCUS:

Do you tell your parents that your friend is using drugs?

DISCUSSION:

1.   Explain your decision.

2.   Are you responsible for your friend's behavior?

3.   Does he become your responsibility because he is in your house?

4. Does loyalty to your friend come before loyalty to your parents?

5. Can you solve this problem and remain loyal to both your friend and your parents?

Dilemma No. 45 — Jr. High and High School

PEACE CORPS CANDIDATE

OBJECTIVE:

To examine a conflict between personal wishes and family responsibilities.

SITUATION:

You are a recent college graduate who has been offered a job with the Peace Corps. You have always wanted to help less fortunate people in other countries, and you enjoy traveling. However, your mother has a severe chronic illness and must stay home most of the time. You are her only child.

FOCUS:

Do you join the Peace Corps?

DISCUSSION:

1. Explain your decision.

2. How do you think you will feel about your choice five years from now?

3. Is it always selfish to put your own wishes first?

4. Can you reach a compromise which will please both of you?

5. Would your decision be different if your mother's doctor said that your mother has less than a year to live? About ten years to live?

9

Writing Your Own Dilemmas

Students and teachers may wish to write original dilemmas. In fact, one of the best ways to engage students in the moral reasoning process is to let *them* identify the problem. The best dilemmas will be the ones students actually encounter in the course of living. If teachers can alert students to what constitutes a dilemma, students won't have to make them up. Dilemmas will happen to them.

Since vicarious experience never makes quite the impression that real experience does, real life moral dilemmas will be more meaningful than made-up ones. An individual's own dilemma will teach him or her more than a neighbor's dilemma will. But students do share common problems, and they will be interested in each other's dilemmas, too. Ultimately, of course, all dilemmas are human dilemmas, and everyone has some kind of stake in them.

Students might be encouraged to carry a sheet of paper in their wallets where they can jot down dilemmas as they realize they are occurring. For example, a student might be in a grocery store with a friend when a friend takes a few grapes from the produce section and pops them in his mouth. His friend hands him some too. Principle and pressure may be conflicting for this student. When he has a chance he makes a note of it, and later he writes it in dilemma form for his class to use.

The teacher can help students recognize dilemmas within the school world, too. A student group is plannimg a boycott of the school cafeteria to protest the poor quality of the food. Should students support the boycott or attempt to work on the problem some other way?

Or perhaps a student feels that a teacher has treated him unfairly. Should he let the air out of the teacher's tires; ask the principal to fire the teacher; talk to the teacher about it after school; arrange a conference between himself, the teacher and his parents; write a letter to the editor of the newspaper; or end it all by dropping out of school?

Clearly, in student's real lives, there are dilemmas. Helping them to recognize them as dilemmas, helping them formulate the focus question, and then helping them identify and evaluate alternatives can be a real service to the student. Not only does it develop a person's moral reasoning and that of the class members who vicariously share the dilemma, it may help the person choose a wiser course of behavior in something that affects him or her immediately.

Sometimes, though, students are too close to certain issues to want to share them. Revealing their own dilemmas can be painful or embarassing. So, students should be encouraged to make up dilemmas. (Frequently, they will express their real concern in fictitous terms.) Students who are writing made-up dilemmas might work from the following topic areas:

Politics, religion, work, leisure time, school, love, sex, family, material possessions, art, music, literature, clothes, hair styles, loyalty, peer group pressure, money, aging—death, health, race, war, peace, rules, laws, authority, courage, persistence, responsibility, cooperativesness, competitiveness, friendship, loyalty, honesty.

Students might use the objectives of the dilemmas in Chapter 8 as bases for additional dilemmas. They also might want to re-write the dilemmas as presented there, or write alternative dilemmas.

If your students do not provide you with sufficient dilemmas, you may want to create your own out of your observations of their lives. Whether you write them or your students do, the following guidelines should assist in the creation of moral dilemmas:

1. Build the dilemma so that a relevant moral or ethical predicament is presented. It should contain a real choice. In order to have cognitive conflict there must be a variety of plausible alternatives and no universal agreement about the issues.

2. When possible, use real-life problems so that the students identify with the setting and situation of the dilemma. Whenever the situation is made-up or involves another time frame, the content must be especially relevant.

3. The story should be simple, interesting and short. Unnecessary details should be excluded.

4. The story should culminate in a decision. Take care to construct a focus question which poses a choice.

5. Make sure the situation is a genuine dilemma and not a story with a moral. If the right answer is obvious, it is not a dilemma. Do not "lead the witness" or indoctrinate.

6.   Ask questions about the choice, the reasons for the choice and alternatives to the choice. Avoid "either—or" or "yes—no" questions. They are dead-ends for discussion. The wording of a question can often be changed to disallow a "yes" or "no" answer.

Writing your own dilemmas can lead the moral reasoning process away from abstractions to the very personal level where people live and decide. It can be the students' opportunity to share their important problems with an interested adult and with each other in a productive way. It can alert them to the presence of dilemmas as they occur in their lives, thus enabling them to practice the reasoning they have learned. The writing and discussing of dilemmas can be a time of significant sharing and learning.

10

Looking Into The Future

In a world situation in which the only certainty is change, we cannot hope to equip students with all of the answers. We cannot even predict most of the questions.

But we can hope that our students will develop habits of mind that will help them cope with both their present and their future. We want our students to be able to face modern complexity with a capacity for making choices.

We used to assume such thinking habits and decision-making ability would come with maturity, that it would develop as naturally and organically as grey hair and wrinkles. But wisdom and adulthood are not achieved simultaneously, as any reader of the newspaper knows.

We used to assume that homes and churches taught morality and values, and that information and skills were the domain of the schools. But our students have many ways of showing us that knowledge and skills and feelings and morality and values are inextricably related to one another in their lives, both in the home and in the school.

So teachers are faced with teaching living, along with reading and arithmetic. As teachers deal more and more with questions than with answers, with processes more than with products, they need new methodologies and new materials. They need new concepts of their own roles and new ways of implementing these roles. It is hoped that this book will help teachers prepare themselves and their students to more successfully live in today *and* tomorrow.

BIBLIOGRAPHY

Beck, Clive. *Moral Education in the Schools*. Toronto, Ontario: The Ontario Institute for Studies in Education, 1971.

Beck, Clive, B.S. Crittenden, and E.V. Sullivan. *Moral Education: Interdisciplinary Approaches*. Toronto, Ontario: The University of Toronto Press, 1971.

Blatt, M., "Studies on the Effects of Classroom Discussion upon Children's Moral Development." Unpublished doctoral dissertation, University of Chicago, 1970.

Brown, George I. *Human Teaching for Human Learning: An Introduction to Confluent Education*. New York: Viking Press, 1971.

Bruner, Jerome S. *Toward a Theory of Instruction*. Cambridge: Harvard University Press, 1966.

Bull, John, *Moral Judgment from Childhood to Adolescence*. London: Routledge and Kegan Paul, 1969

Castillo, Gloria. *Left-Handed Teaching*. New York: Praeger Publishers, 1974.

Craig, Robert. "Lawrence Kohlberg and Moral Development: Some Reflections." *Educational Theory*, Vol. XXIV, No. 2, Spring 1974 pp. 121-129.

Dewey, John. *Moral Principles in Education*. New York: Philosophical Society Library, 1959.

Di Marco, Nicholas. "Life Style, Learning Structures, Congruence and Student Attitudes." *American Educational Research Journal*, Vol. XI, No. 2, Spring 1974, pp.203-209.

Fraenkel, Jack R. *Helping Students Think and Value*. Englewood Cliffs, New Jersey: Prentice-Hall, 1973.

_____. "Values Education in the Social Studies." *Phi Delta Kappan*, Vol. L, No. 9, April 1969, pp. 457-461.

Graham, Richard. "Moral Education: A Child's Right to a Just Community." *Elementary School Guidance and Counseling*, Vol. IX, No. 4, May 1975, pp. 299-308.

Greer, Mary, and Bonnie Rubenstein. *Will the Real Teacher Please Stand Up? A Primer in Humanistic Education*. Pacific Palisades, California: Goodyear Publishing Company, 1972.

Guilford, Joan S. *Development of a Value Inventory for Grades 1-3 in Five Ethnic Groups*. ERIC Document: ED 050 178. Washington, D.C.: U.S. Office of Education, 1971.

Kay, William. *Moral Development.* London: Unwin, 1968.

Kohlberg, Lawrence, and C. Gilligan. "The Adolescent as a Philosopher: The Discovery of the Self in a Post-Conventional World." *Daedalus,* Vol. C, No. 4, Fall 1971, pp. 1051-1086.

Kohlberg, Lawrence. "The Child as a Moral Philosopher." *Psychology Today,* Vol. II, No. 7, September 1968, pp. 25-30.

————. "Collected Papers on Moral Development and Moral Education." Monograph (mimeographed). Cambridge: Harvard University Laboratory of Human Development, 1973.

————. "Comments on the Dilemma of Obedience." *Phi Delta Kappan,* Vol. LV, No. 9, May 1974, p. 607+.

————. "The Concept of Developmental Psychology as the Central Guide to Education," from *Psychology and the Process of Schooling in the Next Decade,* edited by M. Reynalds. Minneapolis: University of Minnesota, Audio-Visual Extension.

————. "Developing the Personal and Religious Maturity." Speech given at N.C.E.A. Convention, April 1974.

Kohlberg, Lawrence, and Rochelle Mayer. "Development as the Aim of Education." *Harvard Educational Review,* Vol. XLII, No. 4, November 1972, pp. 449-496 (and) Vo. XLIII, No. 2, May 1973, pp. 312-314.

Kohlberg, Lawrence. "The Development of Children's Orientation Toward a Moral Order." *Vita Humana,* Vol. VI, 1963.

————. "Development of Moral Character and Moral Ideology." *Review of Child Development Research,* Vol. I. New York: Russell Sage Foundation, 1964.

————. "Education for Justice," from *Moral Education: Five Lectures,* edited by James N. Gustafson. Cambridge: Harvard University Press, 1970.

Kohlberg, Lawrence, "From Is to Ought: How to Commit the Naturalistic Fallacy and Get Away with It in the Study of Moral Development," from *Cognitive Development and Epistemology,* by Theodore Mischel.

————. "Indoctrination Versus Relativity in Value Education." *Zygon,* Vol. VI, No. 4, December 1971, pp. 285-310.

Kohlberg, Lawrence, P. Scharf, and J. Hickey. "The Justice Structure of the Prison - A Theory and an Intervention." *The Prison Journal,* Vol. LI, No. 2, AutumnWinter 1972.

Kohlberg, Lawrence. "Moral and Religious Education and the Public Schools," from *Religion and Public Education,* edited by T. Sizer. Boston: Houghton Mifflin Company, 1966.

Kohlberg, Lawrence, and E. Turiel. "Moral Development and Moral Education," from *Psychology and the Educational Process,* edited by G. Lesser. Chicago: Scott, Foresman, 1971.

Kohlberg, Lawrence. "Moral Development and the New Social Studies." *Social Education,* Vol. XXXVII, No. 5, May 1973, pp. 360-375.

_____. "Moral Education in the Schools: A Developmental View." *School Review,* Vol. LXXIV, No. 1, Spring 1966, pp. 1-29.

_____. "Stage and Sequence: The Cognitive Developmental Approach to Socialization," from *Handbook of Socialization: Theory and Research,* edited by D. A. Goslin. Chicago: Rand, McNally and Company, 1969.

Kohlberg, Lawrence, and Phillip Whitten. "Understanding the Hidden Curriculum." *Learning,* Vol. I, No. 2, December 1972, pp. 10-14.

Krathwohl, David R., and others. *Taxonomy of Educational Objectives, Handbook II: Affective Domain.* New York: David McKay, 1974.

Lawson, David, *The Teaching of Values.* McGill University Press, 1970.

Litchen, Ruth E. *How to Use Group Discussions.* (How to Series, No. 6.). Washington, D.C.: National Council for the Social Studies, 1965.

Lockwood, Alan, and Lawrence Kohlberg. "Cognitive Developmental Psychology and Political Education." Unpublished paper, Harvard University.

Lockwood, Alan. *Moral Reasoning: The Value of Life.* Columbus, Ohio: American Education Publications.

Maslow, Abraham H. *Toward A Psychology of Being.* Princeton, New Jersey: Van Nostrand, 1968.

McBride, A. "Moral Education and the Kohlberg Thesis." *Momentum,* Vol. IV, December 1973.

Miller, Harry G., and Samuel M. Vineur. *A Method for Clarifying Value Statements in the Social Studies Classroom: A Self-Instructional Program.* Washington, D.C.: U.S. Department of Health, Education, and Welfare, Office of Education, 1972.

Moskey, James A. "Moral Insight in the Classrooms." *The Elementary School Journal,* Vol. LXXIII, No. 5, February 1973, pp. 233-238.

Mussen, Paul H. *The Psychological Development of the Child.* Englewood Cliffs, New Jersey: Prentice-Hall 1973.

Piaget, Jean. *The Moral Judgment of the Child.* London: Routledge and Kegan Paul, 1932.

Porter, Nancy. "Kohlberg and Moral Development." *Journal of Moral Education,* Vol. 1, No. 2, 1971.

Rest, James. "Developmental Psychology as a Guide to Value Education: A review of 'Kohlbergian Programs. " *Review of Educational Research,* Vol. XLIV, No. 2, Spring 1974, pp. 241-259.

Rogers, Carl. *Freedom to Learn.* Columbus, Ohio: Charles E. Merrill Publishing Company, 1969.

Shaftel, Fannie R., and George Shaftel. *Role-Playing for Social Values: Decision-Making in the Social Studies.* Englewood Cliffs, New Jersey: Prentice-Hall, 1967.

Simon, Sidney. L. Howe, and H. Kirschenbaum. *Values Clarification: A Practical Handbook of Strategies for Teachers and Students.* New York: Hart Publishing Company, 1972.

Sprinthall, Norman A. "A Program for Psychological Education: Some Preliminary Issues." *Journal of School Psychology,* Vol. IX, No. 4, Winter 1971, pp. 373-382.

Tyler, Ralph. *Basic Principles of Curriculum and Instruction.* Chicago: University of Chicago Press, 1969.

Williams, Norman, and Sheila Williams. *The Moral Development of Children.* London: Macmillan Ltd., 1970.

The Following articles are available for Purchase from the Moral Education and Research Foundation, Roy E. Larson Hall, Appian Way, Harvard University, Cambridge, Massachusetts 02138.

Moral Judgment Interview and Procedures for Scoring. Kohlberg, L., 1971 (Includes articleNo. 13).

Stage and Sequence: The Cognitive-Developmental Approach to Socialization. Kohlberg, L., (Chapter 6 in *Handbook of Socialization Theory,* ed. by D. Goslin. Rand McNally, 1969).

The Child as a Moral Philosopher. Kohlberg, L. (*Psychology Today,* Vol. II, No. 7, September 1968).

A Handbook for Assessing Moral Reasoning. Porter & Taylor.

The Effects of Classroom Moral Discussion Upon Children's Level of Moral Judgment. Blatt, M., and Kohlberg, L. (Chapter 38 in Kohlberg and Turiel, editors. Holt, Rinehart, and Winston, 1973).

Stages of Moral Development as a Basis for Moral Education. Kohlberg, Beck, Crittenden, and Sullivan.

Moral Development and Moral Education. Kohlberg, Turiel, and Lesser, (editor). (*Psychology and the Educational Process.* Chicago: Scott, Foresman, 1971).

From Is to Ought: How to Commit the Naturalistic Fallacy and Get Away with It in the Study of Moral Development. Kohlberg, L. (*Cognitive Development and Epistemology,* by Theodore Mischel. Academic Press, 1971).

The Adolescent as a Philosopher. The Discovery of the Self in a Postconventional World. Kohlberg and Gilligan, C. (*Daedalus,* Journal of the American Academy of Arts and Sciences, 1971).

The Concept of Developmental Psychology as the Central Guide to Education: Examples from Cognitive, Moral and Psychological Education. Kohlberg.

Bureaucratic Violence and Conventional Moral Thinking. Kohlberg, and Scharf, P. (American Journal of Orthopsychiatry).

Continuities in Childhood and Adult Moral Development Revisited. Kohlberg, L. (Chapter 45 in Kohlberg and Turies, editors. Holt, Rinehart, and Winston, 1973).

The Hierarchical Nature of Moral Judgment: a Study of Patterns of Comprehension and Preference of Moral Stages. Rest, James R.

The Justice Structure of the Prison - A Theory and an Intervention. Kohlberg, Scharf, P., and Hickey, J., (The Prison Journal, Vol. LI, No. 2, AutumnWinter 1972).

Moral Judgment and Ego Controls as Determinants of Resistance to Cheating. Krebs, R., and Kohlberg. (Chapter 15 in Kohlberg and Turiel, editors. Holt, Rinehart, and Winston, 1973).

Development as the Aim of Education. Kohlberg and Mayer.

Collected Papers on Moral Development and Moral Education. Kohlberg, L.

Stages and Aging in Moral Development - Some Speculation. Kohlberg, L.

The Claim of Moral Adequacy of a Highest Stage of Moral Judgment. Kohlberg, L.

Developing Senses of Law and Legal Justice. Kohlberg, L.

Education for Justice: A Modern Statement of the Platonic View. Kohlberg, L.

The Implications of Moral Stages for Problems in Sex Education, Kohlberg, L.

BECOMING AWARE OF VALUES by Simpson   Parent/Teacher Resource
Becoming Aware of Values describes a new teaching method and
offers many practical strategies for classroom teachers.
Specific classroom activities are listed. Sample worksheets
and an excellent section on educational games provide the
teacher with ideas to stimulate student participation.
     Valuing is based on the premise that each individual
has basic needs; for example, affection, responsibility,
respect; and that self-esteem depends on the fulfillment of
these basic needs. The Valuing process encourages personal
growth and development, and helps the teacher encourage self-
confidence and a positive self-image in students.
#1801, paper, $4.95

BEGINNING VALUES CLARIFICATION by Simon & Clark   P/T Resource
Beginning Values Clarification step-by-step describes how to
use values clarification in the classroom. It shows how to
help students clarify those things that are important to them.
Teachers will find the suggestions and strategies useful,
practical and stimulating.
1157, paper, $4.95

GETTING IT TOGETHER by Mattox   Parent/Teacher Resource
Getting It Together puts Dr. Lawrence Kohlberg's theories on
moral development into a readily understood teacher's handbook
for use in the classroom. The teacher is provided with
detailed information on working with students in the use of
the peer group discussion of dilemmas. The large number of
dilemmas provided are suitable for use with various age levels,
elementary through high school.
#1814, paper, $4.95

JUMP TO LEARN by Colwell   Parent/Teacher Resource
The Jump To Learn program is based on the premise that
confidence and self-esteem in young children will grow as
they master exercises in coordination and motor skills, such
as skipping rope, catching, throwing or running. As the
children experience success and gain skills, they also learn
to work with other children. It is an indispensible guidebook
for anyone working with young children, Pre-School/Kindergarten
#1821, paper, $6.95

VALUING IN THE FAMILY by Brayer & Cleary   P/T Resource
Valuing in the Family is a workshop guide for parents. It is
designed to help parents implement the Valuing process in the
home, encouraging respect and self-esteem in family relations.
It is written as a guide to help parents understand their
children's needs, and to meet these needs through specific
methods and activities listed in the book. It is used successfully in a growing number of parent workshops throughout the
United States.
#1802, paper, $4.95

For the most complete catalogue currently available of books, games and inventory instruments in values and moral education.

WRITE TO:

"VALUES EDUCATION RESOURCE MATERIALS FOR ALL AGES"
PENNANT EDUCATIONAL MATERIALS
8265 COMMERCIAL STREET #14
LA MESA, CA 92041